The Tablature Writing Book.

Order No. OK 63305
US International Standard Book Number: 0.8256.0187.8
Library of Congress Catalog Card Number: 76–19133

Exclusive Distributors:
Music Sales Corporation
257 Park Avenue South, New York, NY 10010
Music Sales Limited
8/9 Frith Street, London W1V 5TZ England
Music Sales Pty. Limited
120 Rothschild Street, Rosebery, Sydney, NSW 2018, Australia

Printed in the United States of America by
Vicks Lithograph and Printing Corporation

Oak Publications
New York/London/Sydney

Tablature

Tablature is a system of notation in which the lines of the staff represent the strings of the instrument. Each note is indicated by a number which stands for the fret or finger position to be played.

Guitar

The most common application of the tablature concept is for guitar music. Guitar tablature has six lines, the lowest line for the **bass E** and the highest for the **treble E**. A **C chord** would look like this:

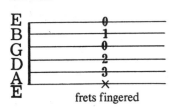

The C Chord

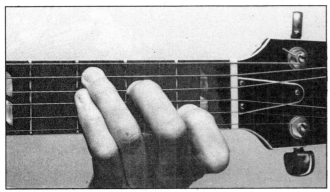

Any note on the guitar neck can be notated in tablature according to its fret position. In the chart below, the notes of each string from the 1st to 12th fret are shown. The appropriate fret number should be written on the line of tablature representing the required string.

A rhythm guitar part, which might consist of block chords, inversions or partial chords, could be written out exactly,

or in block form.

G   C6

Where subdivisions of the beat are necessary, beams and flags can be used.

Various figures can also be shown in tablature.

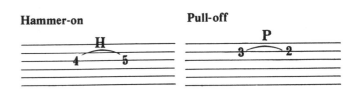

Hammer-on   **Pull-off**

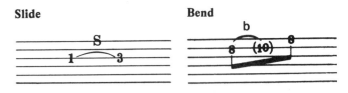

Slide   **Bend**

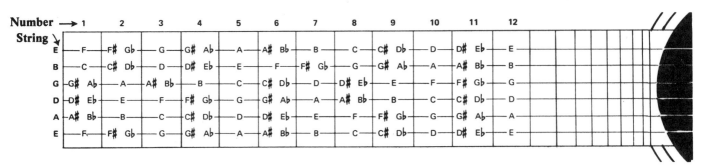

Number →	1	2	3	4	5	6	7	8	9	10	11	12
String ↓												
E	F	F♯ G♭	G	G♯ A♭	A	A♯ B♭	B	C	C♯ D♭	D	D♯ E♭	E
B	C	C♯ D♭	D	D♯ E♭	E	F	F♯ G♭	G	G♯ A♭	A	A♯ B♭	B
G	G♯ A♭	A	A♯ B♭	B	C	C♯ D♭	D	D♯ E♭	E	F	F♯ G♭	G
D	D♯ E♭	E	F	F♯ G♭	G	G♯ A♭	A	A♯ B♭	B	C	C♯ D♭	D
A	A♯ B♭	B	C	C♯ D♭	D	D♯ E♭	E	F	F♯ G♭	G	G♯ A♭	A
E	F	F♯ G♭	G	G♯ A♭	A	A♯ B♭	B	C	C♯ D♭	D	D♯ E♭	E

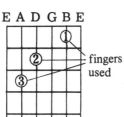

Guitar Chords by Key
Sharp Keys

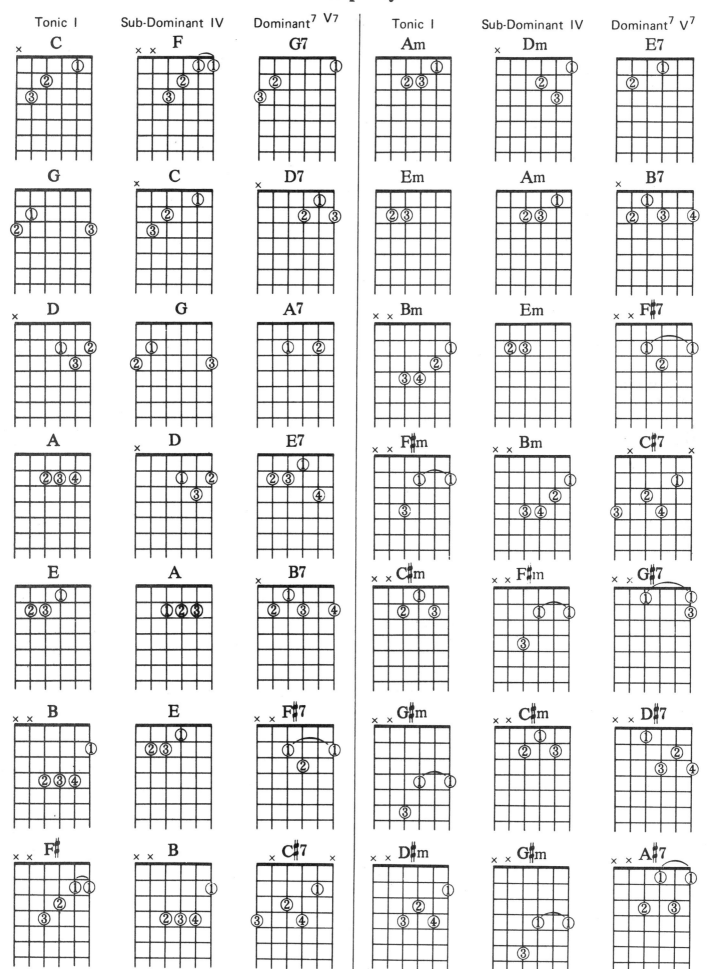

Flat Keys

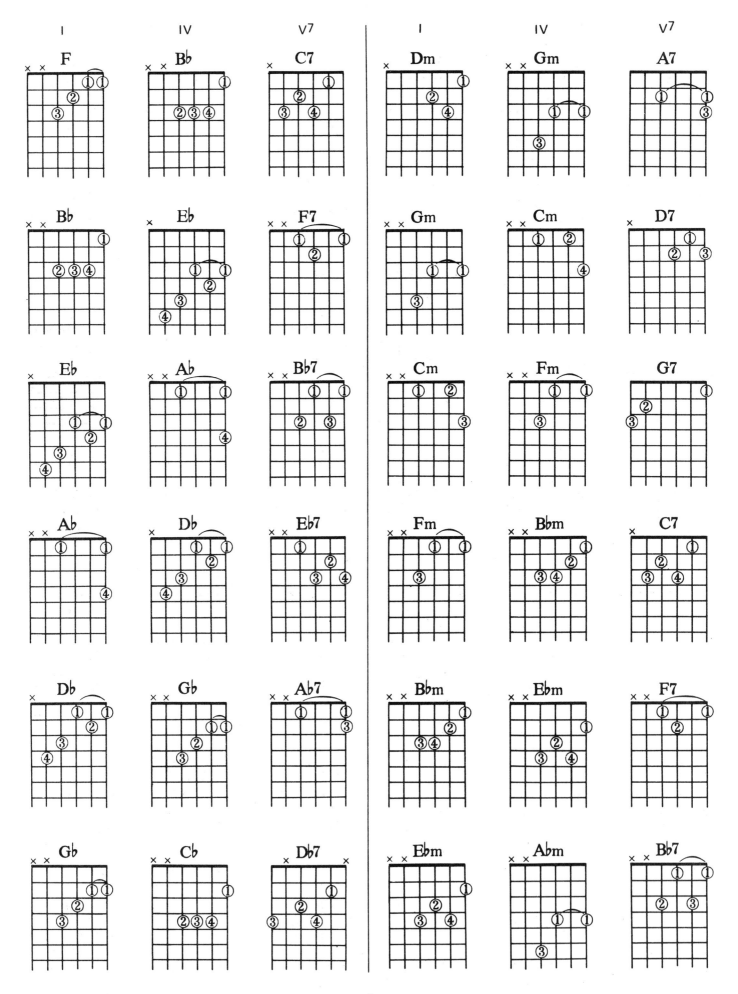

Additional Chord Forms
Sharp Keys

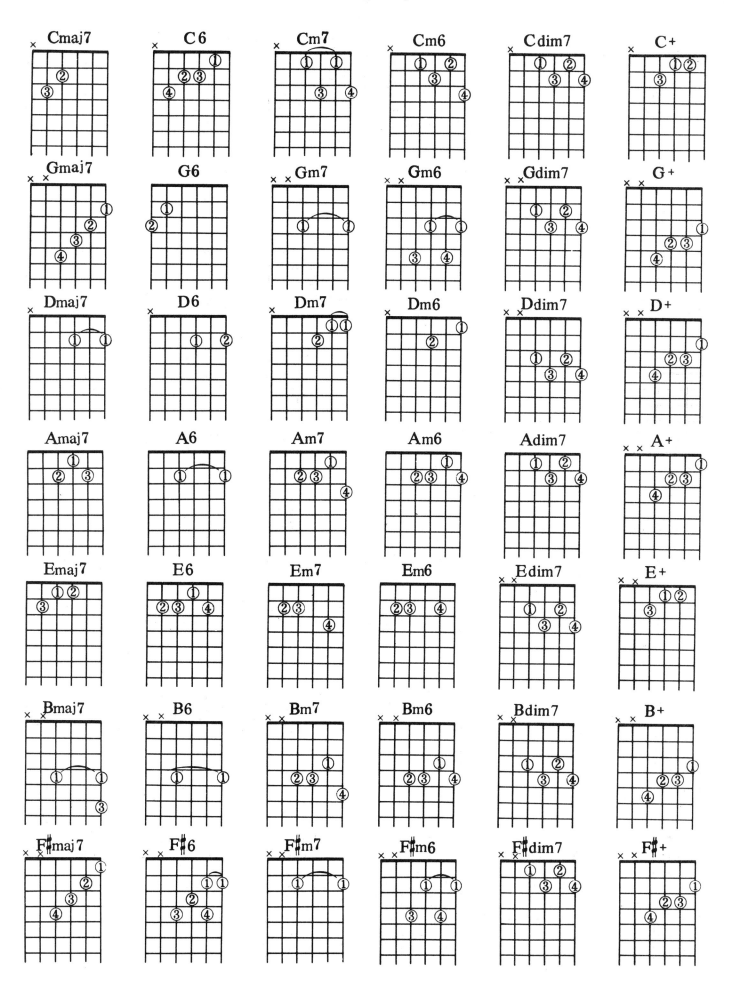

Flat Keys

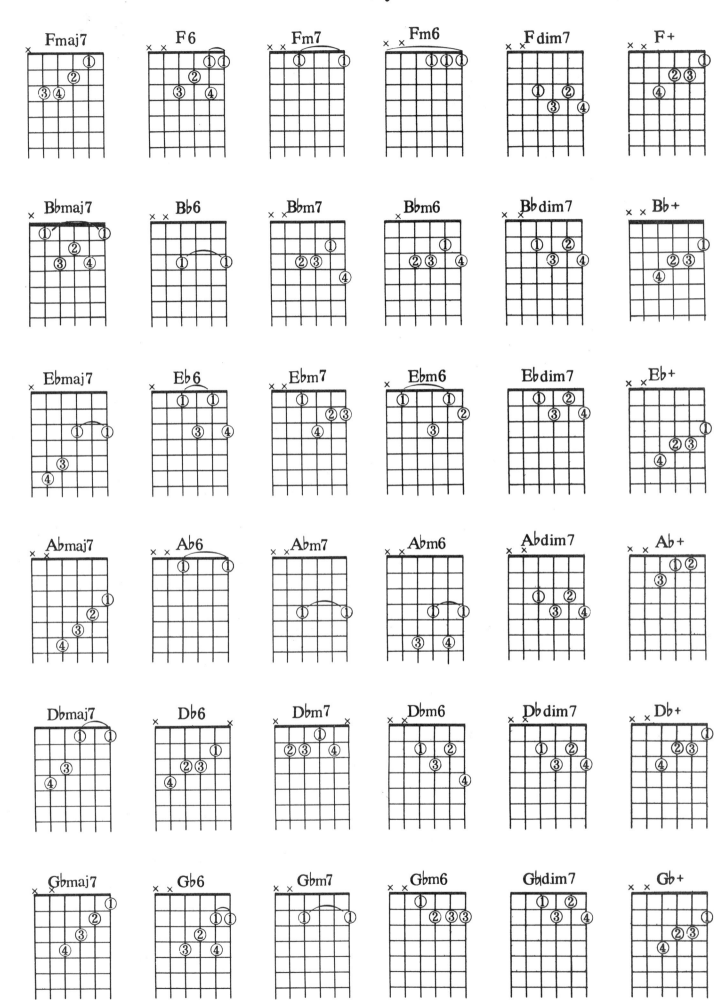

Moveable Chords

Open Tunings

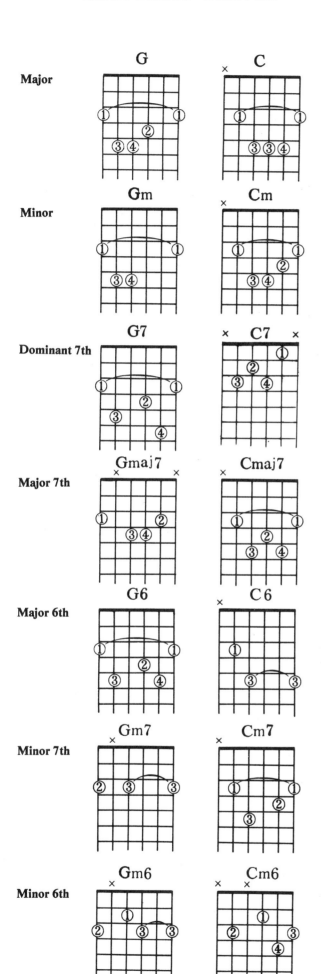

Major — **G**, **C**
Minor — **Gm**, **Cm**
Dominant 7th — **G7**, **C7**
Major 7th — **Gmaj7**, **Cmaj7**
Major 6th — **G6**, **C6**
Minor 7th — **Gm7**, **Cm7**
Minor 6th — **Gm6**, **Cm6**

Chord Positions in
Open E Tuning
(E B E G♯ B E)

Chord positions in
Open G (or A) Tuning
(D G D G B D / E A E C♯ A E)

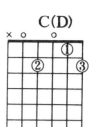

C(D)

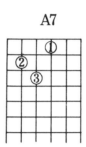

A

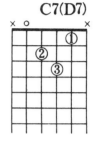

C7(D7)

A7

D(E)

B7

D7(E7)

B

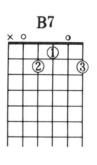

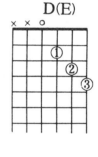

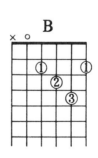

E7

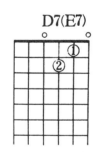

Open Tuning Variations

Dropped D: D A D G B E
Vestapol or Open D:
D A D F♯ A D
Cross-Note: D A D F A D
Spanish, Slack-key or Hawaiian:
D G D G B D
D Modal: D A D G A D

Banjo-style tunings

Open C: C G C G C E
Saw Mill: D G D G C D

7

Banjo

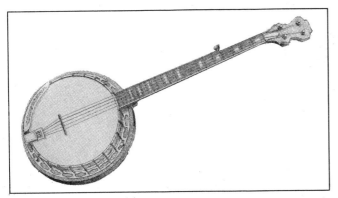

Banjo tunings

Since the banjo has five strings, the spaces between the lines can be used for banjo tablature. As with guitar, the numbers on the staff represent the frets. Numbers below the staff indicate fingerings. A **forward roll** would be written,

and a **backward roll**,

and a "T 1 T 2" roll,

a **hammer-on**, **slide** and **pull-off** are written,

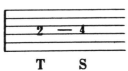

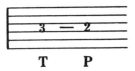

Tablature can be used to indicate any note or chord position.

F Tunings
F tuning ^ADGCD or its variant ^FDGCD

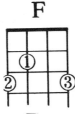 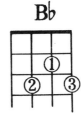 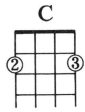

Closely related to this is the tuning ^FDFCD or its variant ^FCFCD. Open dots are used to indicate fretted notes compatible with the tuning.

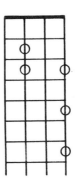

D Tunings
Open D tuning ^{F#}DF[#]AD or its variant ^ADF[#]AD

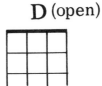

 ←5th   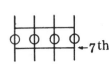 ←7th

Here are two **D tunings** with a minor modal flavor

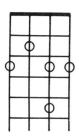 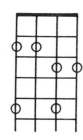

And still a third variant DDGAD

And still a third variant ^{D}DGAD

$^{F\#}$BEAD ^{A}BEAD $^{F\#}$DEAD

D

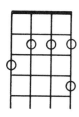 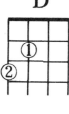 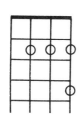

C Tunings
'Standard' C tuning ^{G}CGBD

C   **F**   **G**

  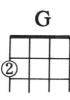 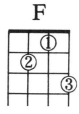

 ←5th   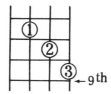 ←7th   ←9th

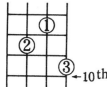 ←10th   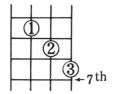 ←10th   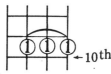 ←12th

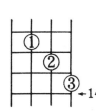 ←14th   **D7**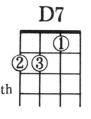   **G7**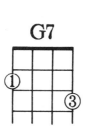

Am

Two **C tunings** ^{G}CGCD

Variant ^{E}CGCD

C   **F**   **G**$+4^{th}$

  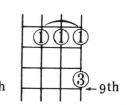

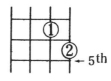 ←5th   ←7th   ←9th

 ←5th

Open **C tuning** ^{G}CGCE

C   **F**   **G**

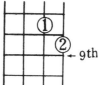

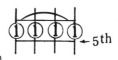 ←9th   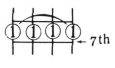 ←5th   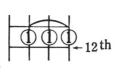 ←7th

^{E}CGAD ^{G}CGAD

D   **C**   **G**

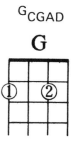 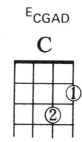 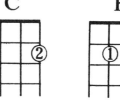 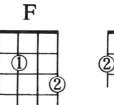

G Tunings
Open G tuning GDGBD

G(open)

C
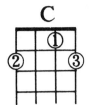

D
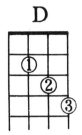

A
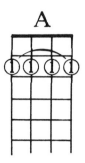

E
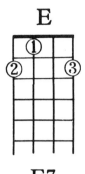

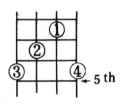

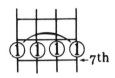

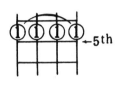

Am
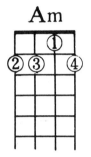

E7
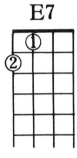

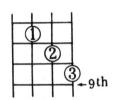

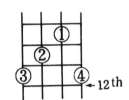

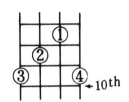

B
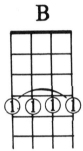

Em
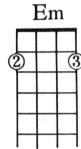

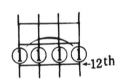

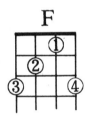

D7

F

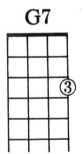

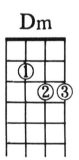

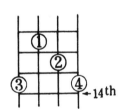

G7

C7

Dm

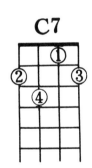

G modal—mountain minor—"sawmill tuning"

^{G}DGCD   variant: ^{G}FGCD

Gm(open)
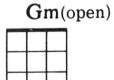

F
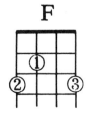

Dulcimer

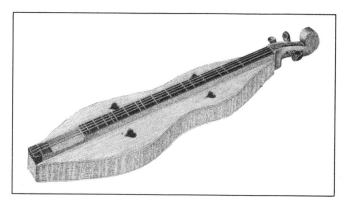

For 4-string dulcimer

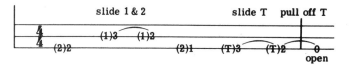

4th : do _____
3rd : sol _____
2nd : do¹ _____
1st : do¹ _____

Numbers refer to fret numbers; 'O' means open string.

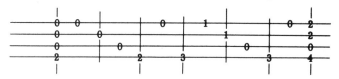

Here are some possibilities for dulcimer notation.

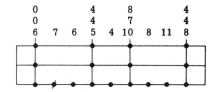

Tuning: do, sol, fa

Dulcimer Tunings

Major Tunings

Key	Open Tuning	Third-fret Tuning
G	G-G-D-G	D-D-G-D
A	A-A-E-A	E-E-A-E
B	B-B-F♯-B	F♯-F♯-B-F♯
C	C-C-G-C	G-G-C-G
D	D-D-A-D	A-A-D-A
E	E-E-B-E	B-B-E-B
F	F-F-C-F	C-C-F-C

Minor Tunings

Key	Open Minor Tuning	Third-String Minor Tuning
G minor	F-G-D-G	C-D-G-D
A minor	G-A-E-A	D-E-A-E
B minor	A-B-F♯-B	E-F♯-B-F♯
C minor	B♭-C-G-C	F-G-C-G
D minor	C-D-A-D	G-A-D-A
E minor	D-E-B-E	A-B-E-B
F minor	E♭-F-C-F	B♭-C-F-C

Mandolin and Fiddle

Fiddles and mandolins are tuned the same way (**GDAE**) and can use the same tablature.

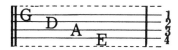

Here is some typical fiddle/mandolin tablature.

Fiddle

Mandolin

Mandolin Neck Chart

Use fret numbers in right hand column for tablature.

	4th OR G	3rd OR D	2nd OR A	1st OR E
	G♯ or A♭ D♯ or E♭	A♯ or B♭	F
	A	E	B	F♯ or G♭
	A♯ or B♭ F	C	G
	B	F♯ or G♭ C♯ or D♭ G♯ or A♭
	C	G	D	A
	C♯ or D♭ G♯ or A♭ D♯ or E♭ A♯ or B♭
	D	A	E	B ←7th fret

11

Mandolin Chord Chart

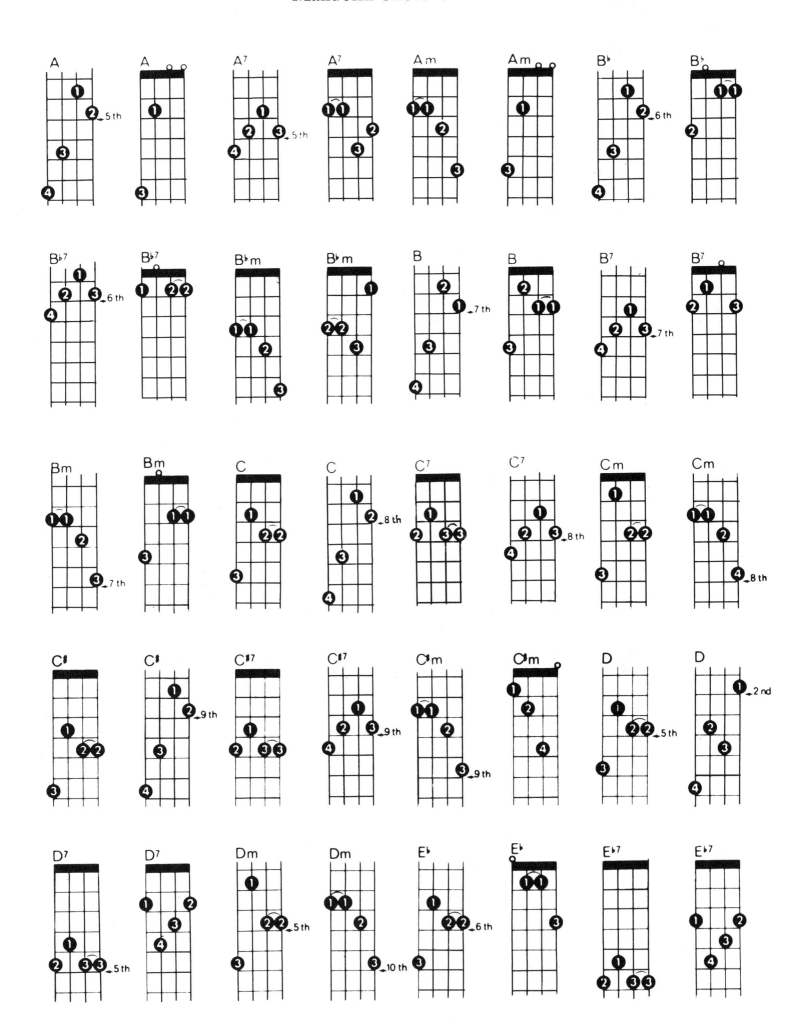

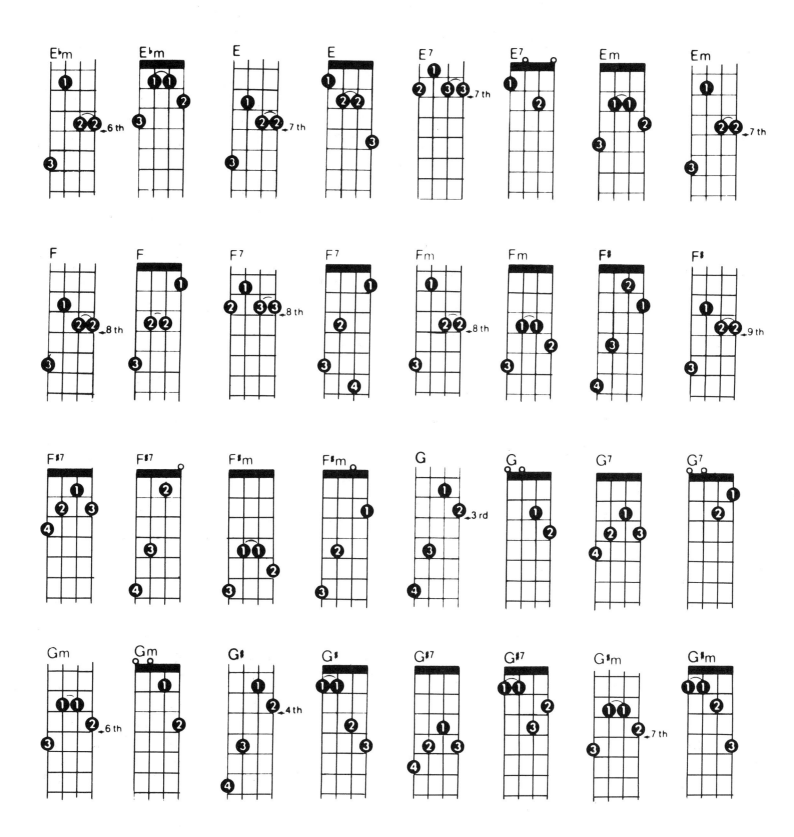

Bass Guitar

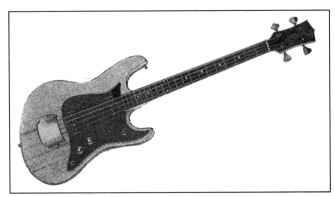

Bass guitar tablature requires only four lines for the four bass strings. A typical bass line looks like this.

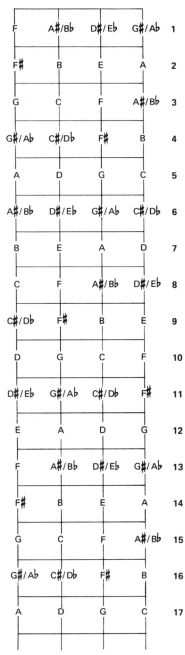

Bass Neck Chart/Tablature Guide

Numbers at the right provide tablature reference.

	E	A	D	G	
1	F	A#/Bb	D#/Eb	G#/Ab	1
2	F#	B	E	A	2
3	G	C	F	A#/Bb	3
4	G#/Ab	C#/Db	F#	B	4
5	A	D	G	C	5
6	A#/Bb	D#/Eb	G#/Ab	C#/Db	6
7	B	E	A	D	7
8	C	F	A#/Bb	D#/Eb	8
9	C#/Db	F#	B	E	9
10	D	G	C	F	10
11	D#/Eb	G#/Ab	C#/Db	F#	11
12	E	A	D	G	12
13	F	A#/Bb	D#/Eb	G#/Ab	13
14	F#	B	E	A	14
15	G	C	F	A#/Bb	15
16	G#/Ab	C#/Db	F#	B	16
17	A	D	G	C	17

Recommended Tuition Material

The Complete Guitar Player Book 4 – Russ Shipton (Amsco)
Folk Guitar Styles Of Today Books 1 & 2 – Russ Shipton (Oak)
The Folksinger's Guide to the Classical Guitar – Harvey Vinson (Oak)
Slide Guitar – Arlen Roth (Oak)
Finger-picking Styles for Guitar – Happy Traum (Oak)
Lead Guitar – Harvey Vinson (Amsco)
Bluegrass Banjo – Peter Wernick (Oak)
Clawhammer Banjo – Miles Krassen (Oak)
Melodic Banjo – Tony Trischka (Oak)
Bluegrass Mandolin – Jack Tottle (Oak)
Bluegrass Fiddle – Gene Lowinger (Oak)
Appalachian Fiddle – Miles Krassen (Oak)
The Dulcimer Book – Jean Ritchie (Oak)
Bass Guitar – Jim Gregory & Harvey Vinson (Amsco)

Available at your local music store or from Music Sales Corporation, 24 East 22nd Street, New York, N.Y. 10010. Write for FREE catalog.

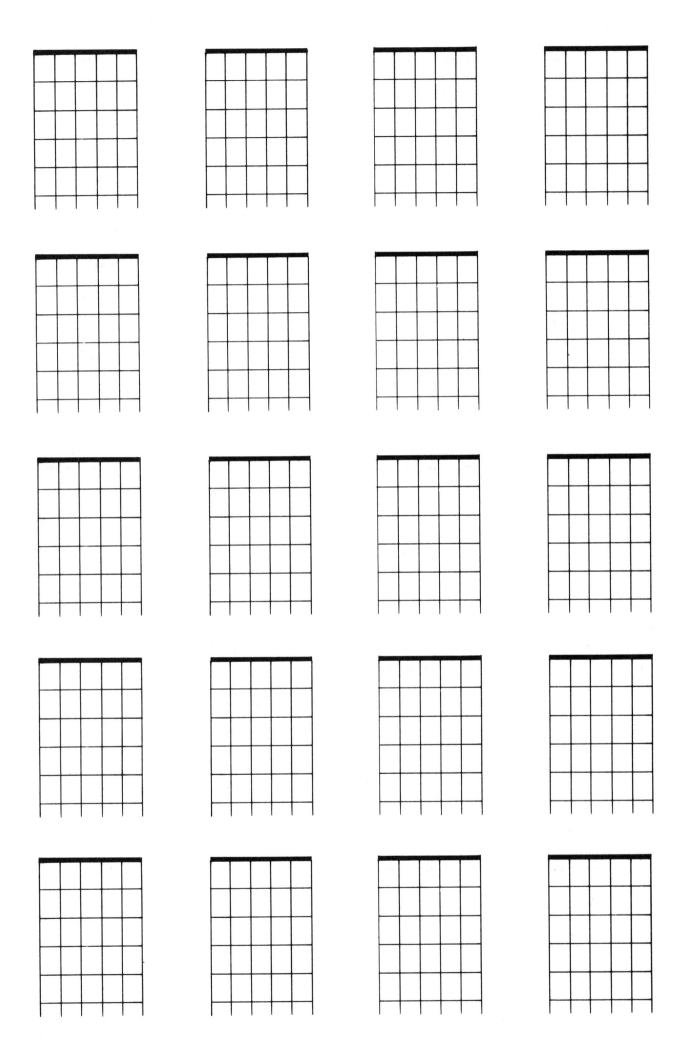

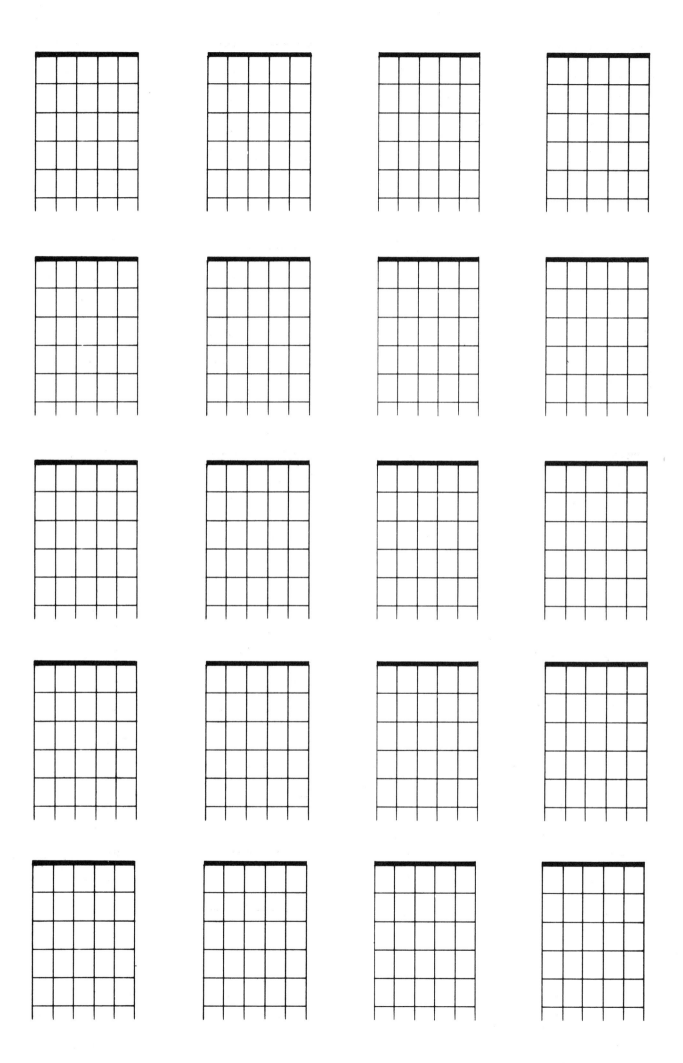

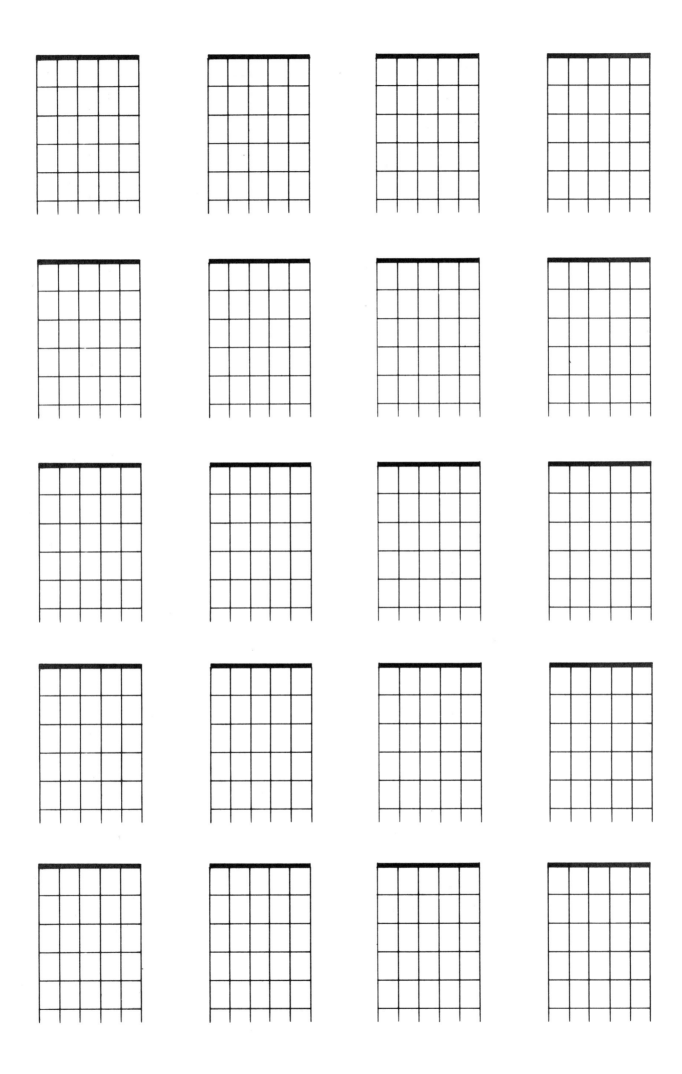

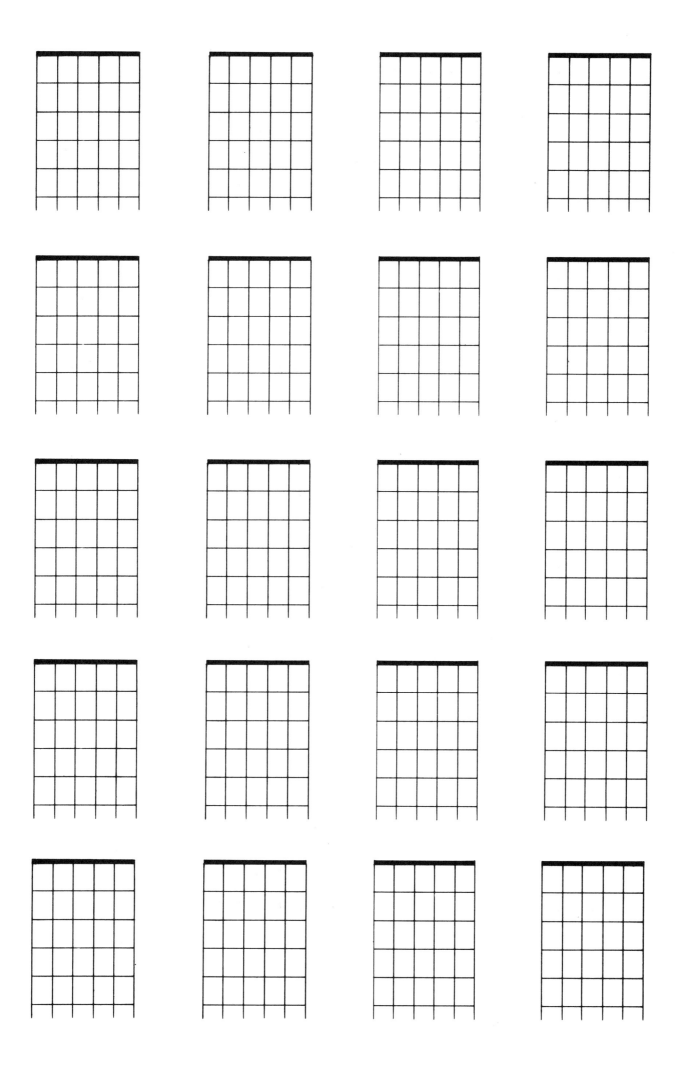

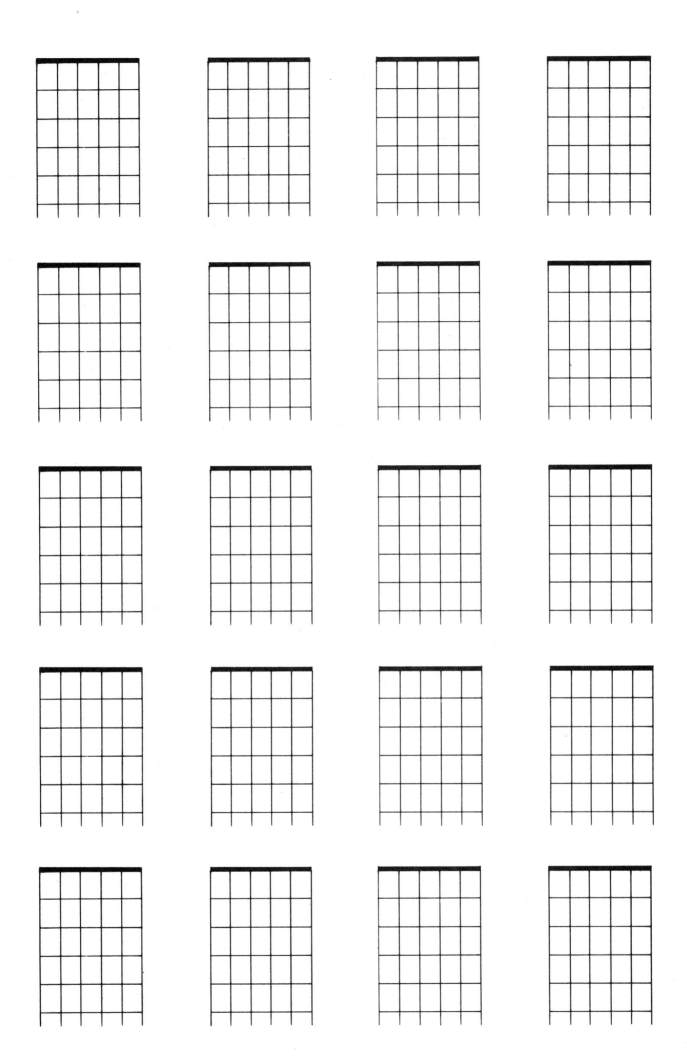